Knowing Jesus...

By Dr. John S. Peters

Copyright © 2012
by John Peters (RevDr J S Peters)

Knowing Jesus
Rev. Dr. J S Peters Talks About Knowing Jesus
by John Peters (RevDr J S Peters)

Printed in the United States of America

ISBN 9781624195747

All rights reserved solely by the author. The author guarantees all contents are original and do not infringe upon the legal rights of any other person or work. No part of this book may be reproduced in any form without the permission of the author. The views expressed in this book are not necessarily those of the publisher.

Unless otherwise indicated, Bible quotations are taken from The King James Version of the Bible; The HOLY BIBLE, NEW INTERNATIONAL VERSION®. NIV®. Copyright © 1973, 1978, 1984 by International Bible Society. Used by permission of Zondervan; and The Holy Bible, New Living Translation NLT. Copyright © 1996. Used by permission of Tyndale House Publishers, Inc., Wheaton, Illinois 60189.

www.xulonpress.com

Contents

Preface vii

Part One: A Divine Intervention 11

   Chapter One 13

   Chapter Two.................................. 27

   Chapter Three................................ 43

   Chapter Four................................. 54

   Chapter Five 59

   Chapter Six 67

   Chapter Seven 73

Part Two: Taking the Right Exit........... 85

   Chapter Eight................................. 87

   Chapter Nine................................. 95

Chapter Ten 120

Chapter Eleven 152

Preface

𝒫raise The Lord! I am excited with what God is doing in these last days. Everywhere I look, I see the signs of His coming as foretold in the written Word of God, the Holy Scriptures, otherwise known as the Holy Bible. I say it in this fashion, because this book is written to the unbeliever, as much as it is written to the believer.

The very last thing Jesus said to His disciples before He ascended back into heaven was this: "But you shall receive power when the Holy Spirit comes upon you. And you shall be my witnesses, telling people about me everywhere … in Jerusalem, throughout Judea, in Samaria, and to the ends of the earth."

You may read this book, and try to figure out "where I am coming from." If you do, you'll miss it. Allow me to say this much about myself: I am a witness to our Lord Jesus Christ. My purpose in writing this book is simply to tell people everywhere about what I have seen Jesus doing in the world today. My desire is to share the written Word of God and to try to help someone to understand the simplicity of the gospel of Christ.

My name is Bishop J. S. Peters, and I have been a minister of the gospel of our Lord Jesus Christ for over twenty years. Every day that passes brings me some new revelation of the goodness of our Father in heaven. Each day, I see the Word of God fulfilled, proven to be true and accurate. Throughout my ministry, I have seen many signs, wonders, and miracles. I have seen short limbs grow out, deaf ears and blind eyes opened, arthritis and diabetes cast out, and incurable pain healed instantly. I have seen people receive money miracles, be delivered from drug and alcohol abuse, and have even seen the dead raised wonderfully back to life.

In the following pages, I will do my best to be a faithful witness to our Lord and Savior by sharing many testimonies of the things that I have seen God doing in the world through the name of Jesus

Christ, who is the only begotten Son of God, and by the power of the Holy Spirit. I hope you will enjoy reading these pages as much as I have enjoyed writing them.

Part One

A Divine Intervention

Chapter One

*A*s you know already, every book, both the good and the not so good, needs to have three things. It needs a beginning and an end and the rest of the story in between. Very much like a good sandwich, the beginning and the end are the bread and butter, which serve as the foundation for the story. What is in between, serves as the rest of the story, the meat, lettuce, and tomato, or whatever else the maker would care to put into it.

Jesus Himself used many illustrations in order to create mental pictures for His followers and listeners. A good sermon on a Sunday morning will have something for every man, woman, and child to "feed" on, or to think about, through the following week.

While this book is meant to point to and glorify God, I have chosen to use my own testimony to show forth some of what I see God doing from day to day. Today, people will look at me and see someone who is somewhat educated and whose life is free of the influence of drugs and alcohol, a leader in the house of God, which is the church. No one will see the angry young man I used to be. They won't see the derelict street person I used to be. They won't see the young

Chapter One

man whose life was ruined by drugs and alcohol and everything else that went with that lifestyle.

What they will see (whether they recognize it or not) is the miracle God has worked in my life, through the power of the gospel of Christ. You see, when you really "hear" the gospel, it will change your life forever. A transformation takes place that no one can miss or deny.

This is why the gospel is preached to the poor, so that they will see and hear the truth. These people desperately need to recognize the reality and the desperateness of their situation. They need to realize and understand that only God can truly help and save them. When they realize that their only hope is in accepting the person and lordship of Jesus Christ, when they turn their lives over to Christ, knowing in their hearts that they can't make it without His help, their lives are suddenly and wonderfully changed forever.

You might say in your heart, "Oh yeah, here we go again. Listen, pal, I know all about this religion crap. I know all about God and Jesus and the church. I know the Ten Commandments. I go to church, sometimes." Well, maybe you do go to church, maybe you do know about God, Jesus, and the devil. But even the demons believe and tremble. It is not enough to know about God—not since Jesus came on the scene. Maybe you do know the Ten Commandments, but let me ask you this: Do you live by them, or merely follow them as a rough guideline when it is convenient to do so?

Do you understand the purpose God had in mind when He gave us the commandments? They were not given to be a rough guideline so that if we followed them as best we could we would make it into heaven. If you think you must keep the law in one point, you must keep the whole law, and not just the Ten Commandments but also all of the 380-odd laws that were given by Moses. By the same token, if you break the law in one point, you are guilty of breaking all of the law.

They (the Ten Commandments) were given to show sinful man his need for God's mercy and grace. They were given to point the way to God's salvation: Jesus Christ. Like it or not, believe it or not,

Jesus died on the cross to pay the price for sin once and for all. Maybe you are the worst sinner on the face of the earth. Maybe you are a confirmed backslider and you love the world more than anything or anyone. Or maybe you try to be, and are, a truly good person.

The truth is, if you are in this world without Christ in your heart, you are living in sin. How can I say this? What do I know about it? I know what the Word of God has to say about it.

What is sin? Sin is disobedience to God. Anything that is not of faith is sin (Romans 14:23). If a man knows to do right and does it not, to him it is sin. All unrighteousness is sin (1 John 5:17).

Chapter One

If we are in this world without Christ in our hearts, then we are separated from God by the very nature of sin.

The apostle Paul, speaking under the inspiration of the Holy Spirit, makes this clear for us in Romans 5:12-21 (NLT): "When Adam sinned, sin entered the entire human race. Adam's sin brought death, so death spread to everyone, for everyone sinned. Yes, people sinned even before the law was given." But it was not counted as sin because there was not yet any law to break. Still, everyone died—from the time of Adam to the time of Moses—even those who did not break any explicit commandment of God, as Adam did.

Now Adam is a symbol, a representation of Christ, who was yet to come.

But there is a great difference between Adam's sin and God's gracious gift. For the sin of this one man, Adam, brought death to many. But even greater is God's wonderful grace and his gift of forgiveness to many through this other man, Jesus Christ. "And the result of God's gracious gift is very different from the result of that one man's sin. For Adam's sin led to condemnation" (v. 16), but God's free gift leads to our being made right with God, even though we are guilty of many sins.

The sin of this one man, Adam, caused death to rule over many. But even greater is God's wonderful grace and his gift of righteousness, for all who receive it will live in "triumph over sin and death through this one man, Jesus." Yes, Adam's one sin brings condemnation upon everyone, but Christ's one act of righteousness" (vv. 17-18) brings a right relationship with God and a new life for everyone. "Because one person disobeyed God, many [or all] became sinners. But because one other person [Jesus] obeyed God many" (v. 19) [as many as will receive Jesus] will be made righteous.

"God's law was [is] given so that all people could see how sinful they were [are]. But as people sinned more and more, God's wonderful kindness became more abundant. So just as sin ruled over all people and brought them to death, now God's wonderful kindness rules instead, giving us right standing with God and resulting in eternal life through Jesus Christ our Lord" (vv. 20-21).

What all of that means, in a nutshell, is that through the sin of Adam, all people were born into the nature of sin. Through the shed blood of Jesus, who died to pay the price for all of our sins, all who receive Him into their hearts are made clean and receive a new life and right standing with God. Yes, as the Word tells us, the wages (or reward) of sin is death. Each one of us, from Adam until Jesus returns to rule and reign on the earth, is born with a death sentence.

Jesus paid that price for each of us, and so the gospel of Christ is preached everywhere so that as many people as possible can receive their full pardon, from the highest court anywhere.

Don't say in your hearts that Jesus is just a crutch for society. Don't play games

Chapter One

with God. Don't play Russian roulette with your spiritual well-being. Don't say, "Eat, drink, and be merry for tomorrow we die." You're already dead.

Jesus left his throne and glory in heaven, lived a perfect life, died on the cross to pay for your sin and mine, rose again on the third day, and ascended back into heaven, after instructing the disciples for forty days.

The Word of God says today is the day of salvation. If you hear His voice, don't harden your hearts as the Israelites did in the wilderness (Hebrews 3:15). This might be the only (or last) chance you have. Let me tell you, young men. Listen to me, young women; heaven is real, and hell is hot. God loves you. It's not too late. There is nothing you have said or done that is so terrible that God can't or won't forgive you.

When Nicodemus, a great leader and respected teacher in the Jewish faith, came to Jesus by night saying, "Teacher … we all know that God has sent you to teach us. Your miraculous signs are proof enough that God is with you," Jesus knew where this speech was leading (John 3:2 NLT).

> Jesus replied, "I assure you, unless you are born again, you cannot see the Kingdom of God."
>
> "What do you mean?" exclaimed Nicodemus. "How can an old man go back into his mother's womb and be born again?"

Chapter One

Jesus replied, "The truth is, no one can enter the Kingdom of God without being born of water and the Spirit. Humans can produce only human life, but the Holy Spirit gives new life from heaven. So don't be surprised at my statement that you must be born again."

John 3:3-6 (NLT)

So, then, what Jesus was saying to one of the top religious leaders of His day was this: "If you want to be saved, if you want to make heaven your home for all eternity, you must be born again. I tell you this because you are physically alive, but you are spiritually dead, because of the sin nature within you. Be water baptized for the remission of sins, and then you can be born of the Holy Spirit and adopted into the family of God."

Chapter Two

*I*n this world, when a man and a woman have children before they are married, once they do marry and make it right in the eyes of God and man, the father of the children has to legally adopt each child, before he can legally give them his name. You might ask me, "What do you know about it?"

I know enough. There was a time in my life when I could not believe that there was a God in heaven. I thought that the name of Jesus and the whole Christianity thing was just a crutch for weak-minded people living in an increasingly decadent society. People would try to preach Jesus and salvation at me; and after talking to me for ten or fifteen minutes, they would walk away, shaking their heads and sometimes even throwing their Bibles in the nearest trash can.

Since that time, I have come to know that I know that He is real and that He is a rewarder of those who diligently seek Him (Hebrews 11:6). To meet and talk with me, you would never know that I was not raised in a Christian home. You would think that all of my life I had been sheltered in the safe embrace and environment of the church and the Christian community. But I was born into, and grew up in, an alcoholic, abusive, and totally dysfunctional environment.

How bad was it? It was bad enough for God to have to intervene. It was bad enough that I still carry the outward scars of moving from one foster home to another. It was bad enough that it took years for God to heal the emotional scars. It was just simply, bad enough.

I thank God that even before I was formed in the womb, God knew me; and by the time I was born, He already had a plan and purpose for me.

Psalm 68:6, tells us that God sets the "solitary in families." Even though I had my older brother with me, I always felt alone in this world. And so I am grateful for that. Even though my foster parents were not perfect, God was still working in me and moving me toward some distant goal that only He could see.

My first experience with the church came when I was maybe eight years old, or even younger. It was just down the street from where I lived at the time, at the First United Church in White Rock, British Columbia. To a young boy, the dim lighting, somber music, and the standard dress of the people did not make a good first impression. "Who died?" was the first thing on my mind, quickly followed by my locating the nearest exit. I may well have bolted had the song not come to an end, at which point the children were sent downstairs for Sunday school.

Where the atmosphere upstairs had seemed kind of eerie, things were much better down here. There were tables and

Chapter Two

chairs, books and crayons, and many other trappings that set my mind at ease, making me feel much more comfortable. There was a young woman running things down here, and she had a pleasant voice. She talked for a while and then asked us this question: "Who would like to have a rich man come and live in your house and bring lots of presents for everyone?"

Well, if you know anything about kids, it should be no surprise that as soon as she mentioned presents, every kid in the place had his or her hand up in the air without hesitation. I did not realize until I was much older that this had in fact been an invitation to accept Christ into our hearts. I have often wondered if this was not what made the way for God to spare my life several years later when three young men had me in a graveyard in the middle of nowhere, intent on taking my life in some crazy kind of ritual thing.

In my mid-twenties, I did something I had never imagined doing, not even in my wildest dreams. I moved away from the lower mainland of beautiful British Columbia to southern Saskatchewan, with its hot summers and very cold winters. Looking back at this move, I can now see that the hand of God had begun to do a new work in my life.

At that point in time, all I knew was that winter was coming and I had to get out of there before it got any colder. In truth, it took about five years for me to become acclimatized to the harsh prairie winters. I would be fine until the mercury dropped to minus 20 Celsius. With the snow flying

Chapter Two

in with a wind from the frozen northlands, I would be on the first Greyhound back to the Vancouver area. It was on one of these migrational journeys that I first recognized the hand of almighty God actively and openly at work.

I had been visiting some very old friends whom I had not really visited for well over a year or more. I guess it would be right to say that we had been partying for most of the night. I left my friends sometime around midnight, dreading the long walk home, if I wasn't able to thumb a ride. It was roughly three miles to the main highway, and maybe another eight or ten after that. It was no small relief to me that the first car to come along slowed, pulled to the side, and waited for me to climb in, as the rear-passenger side door opened, welcoming me inside.

Inside the car, a late model Chevy, were three young men about my own age. Everything seemed to be all right as I eased back into the seat. That is to say that they looked like ordinary young men on their way home from a party, or just a group of young men who had nothing better to do than cruise the highways in order to kill some time.

Thankfully, there wasn't a lot of talk, just a question or two like, how was I doing, and what was I up to? Then they said, "Well, we'll take you anywhere you want to go, but you've got to come smoke a joint with us first." At this point the warning lights began to flicker on, so I told them, "Thanks, but I'm trying to cut

Chapter Two

down." This was really just a polite way of saying, "I'd rather not."

Then they said, "Well, that's OK, but you have to have a drink with us then." Something just didn't feel right at this point, and now the warning lights were burning bright. I knew that this was a bad ride. I didn't let on that I knew something was up, and responded by saying something like, "That's cool. Whatever." We rode on in silence for some time, and then I began to feel something else at work. I know now that it was the Holy Ghost, telling me that I would be all right. All I knew at the time was that suddenly I had a feeling that I would walk away from this one.

Well, they turned left at 152nd Street and went past my home and then turned north onto 72nd Avenue. The driver began to recite some verses about how a man goes into the grave and never comes out, and then he wheeled his vehicle into the graveyard. All three of them jumped out of the car as soon as it came to a full stop. As I made to get out also, they stopped me and said, "You have to wait in the car until we are ready."

I had to shake my head a little over that one. I mean, really? OK, I had had a few drinks and popped a bunch of painkillers, but I wasn't that out of it. I was thinking, "Well, this could prove to get interesting." That was proven true a moment later. They had opened the trunk by now and were quietly discussing something as I peered through the gap under the trunk lid. As I looked, I saw the driver slip a

Chapter Two

machete up his sleeve, and then a bottle of hard stuff was passed around and then placed back in the trunk, which was then slammed shut, and I was allowed to get out of the car.

The driver told me that I would have to wait at the back of the car while he and another discussed something at the front of the car. As you may have noticed, the bottle had been placed back in the trunk of the car, and they had not offered me a drink. How rude! I felt like telling them that they could break it out again when they were done, but I kept quiet.

Instead, I focused my full attention on the third guy, who had stayed at the rear of the car with me. As I leaned back against the rear fender, he squared off in a cheap little karate stance, like I wouldn't know what was coming next. Under ordinary circumstances, I would have let this all go and just walked away. But this was strike three for these guys. So when the karate guy said something rude about my mother, I was ready to give as good as I got. I told him that the same thing could be said for his mom, and he popped me a good one, catching me right on the point of the chin, which rocked my head back a bit. Now, I'm sure that if these guys had known anything about me at all, they would have just given me the promised drink, let me go on my merry way, and gone looking for easier prey.

First of all, I had an older brother who was connected to a number of motorcycle clubs, and if these guys had touched me, he would have had their heads for tro-

Chapter Two

phies. (I want to talk about my brothers some more a little later.) Second, in my own right, I had several years of military training, including two or three years of martial arts. The final thing to consider here is that because of the poor condition of my teeth, I was constantly eating a lot of painkillers. These guys could have hit me with a Mack truck, and I wouldn't have felt a thing.

I have to share a little more about my older brother for a moment, so that I can go on with my story. He was my protector. Just before we went our separate ways, he gave me a tattoo so that everybody would know who I was and would also know that anyone who tried to touch me would have him to deal with.

The reason I feel it necessary to share this is because I learned that I had another big brother (Jesus) who also had put a mark on me and also was looking out for me. I may never know exactly what this poor guy saw when he hit me, but you could have put that scene in a Hollywood movie. His eyes bugged out, his jaw dropped open, he got a funny look on his face, and he turned away, saying, "Oops!" And then he walked gingerly away to tell his friends that they needed a plan B and C.

Up to this point, there had been a chill breeze blowing. Now it stopped abruptly, and it became suddenly warm. This was quickly followed by the air being charged with electricity, like standing under power lines carrying a million volts or more.

Chapter Two

(This is a creative way for me to say that the air was buzzing and crackling with power.) Then it seemed like someone was standing beside me, asking, "What are you waiting for?"

Well, I looked over at these guys, who by now seemed to have forgotten all about me. They were standing near the front of the car (two of them now wearing black robes I might add). I looked around the other way and saw a small patch of evergreen forest about a hundred yards behind me. I looked back at my would-be assailants, shrugged my shoulders, and walked away. I was twenty yards away from the trees before they realized that I had moved an inch.

This was my first real encounter with the presence of God. I later learned that it was Jesus Himself who was standing beside me. I came to know that He had put His mark on me years earlier and had a plan and a purpose for me and was not about to let anybody do me any harm.

Chapter Three

*M*any years later, a guy tried to take my fingers off in a press clamp in order to ruin my music ministry. This was not some unsaved Philistine but rather an elder in one of the local churches! I had come to the Greater Vancouver area to take some training with 100 Huntley Street. My first priorities were to find a place to call home, find a church, and find the local office for Huntley Street.

It was easy to find a light housekeeping room that fit my budget, and it didn't take long to find a church, as well as the ministry offices. At the church, I was befriended by a cheerful young man who was more than happy to help me find my way around. He was involved with a home group in the Lougheed area and wasted no time in introducing me.

For several weeks, the man who owned the home would just stare at me, watching me like a hawk. It didn't matter if we were at the church or at his home, I would always see him watching my every move. When he finally did speak to me, it was not at all how I had expected things to go. He didn't even introduce himself. He just walked up to me and said, "I have

Chapter Three

---

a demon in my shop. I want you to come and work for me and cast it out."

I really didn't know whether to take him seriously or not, so I smiled and promised him that I would pray about it. Some six weeks later, I still had not found other employment, so I gave this brother a call and said that I would try it for a while and see how things went. He had a nice little setup. It was a larger shop that was semi-automated, so that two men could run it efficiently. Well, I worked that first day and didn't notice anything out of the ordinary, except for one corner of the place that seemed to be a little dark and oppressive.

I didn't get any dreams or visions from the Lord that night, but when I got up to go to work the next morning, I got hit with a bleeding ulcer. When I first realized what was happening, I purposed in my heart to go to the hospital. God said, "No, you are going to work." So we argued about it for a while; that is to say, I argued, and God had His way.

I was sure I was looking pretty washed out, so to keep my boss from thinking I had been doing drugs or something, I told him I had lost a "little" blood that morning. God's hand was on me for the next three days, and I worked harder than I had for many years previously. On the morning of the third day, while the big loading door was open on a sunny morning in April or May, I felt the peace of God flood the place. As I looked up to see what was happening, I saw the glory cloud rolling

Chapter Three

into the shop, and that feeling of oppression was gone.

It turned out that the house group was meeting that night, and I was happy to be in a service. One of the first things that happened was that one of the leaders of this group handed me an envelope with a hundred dollars or more. This happened because the Holy Spirit had sent me to his home one morning with a message. He told me that when the word came to pass, I would know it. This was the man's way of showing me that God had honored His word.

The following morning I tried to get dressed and ready for work, but as soon as I stood on my feet, what little blood I had left in me drained down into my legs, causing me to black out and end up on the floor. If I lay down, I was fine. If I tried to stand up, boom!

After about two hours of trying to use my faith to get me to work, I gave it up, called the boss, and told him what was happening with me. An hour later, they took me to the emergency room of a local hospital.

The nurses took one look at me and brought out a wheelchair, saying, "You'll be staying with us for a while, Mr. Peters." It took them from 9:00 a.m. to 10:00 p.m. to get me stabilized. It was then apparent to me that God had taken His hand off of me and said, "Now you can go to the hospital." The Holy Spirit did some other things while I was in the hospital, and word spread around various areas of the hospital, which resulted in several people

Chapter Three

coming to my bedside to receive prayer and ministry.

My employer was so impressed with what God had done that he came to me when I was back on the job, saying, "I am a journeyman cabinetmaker. I want you to make a four-year commitment to me, in which time I will teach you my trade, and then I will sell you my business."

I have to confess that I wanted to accept this offer. However, when I went to prayer about it, the Holy Spirit said, "No, Son, I want you working for Me." I went before the Lord three times, each time with the same result.

When I told my employer that I could not accept his offer, he looked me straight in the eye and without blinking said, "All right, then. I'm going to destroy your ministry." And he walked away.

A few weeks later (after I had forgotten all about his threat), I looked up one day from what I was doing and saw him struggling with a big, oversized cabinet. He called for me to help him get it loaded into the press clamp, and he positioned my hands saying, "Hold it just like that, and don't let go of it for nothing. I have to get the rubber mallet off of the workbench."

I didn't think anything of it and quickly got lost in thinking about the goodness of God. As soon as I had taken my eyes off of him, my boss reached out and flipped on the power switch to activate the machine, trapping my fingers in place. As I stood looking at my fingers and saying to

Chapter Three

myself, "Well, Lord, there goes my music career," the Lord was at my side once more, saying, "No, John. You're fine." I responded quickly by saying, "Lord, I'll receive that report!"

I looked at my boss then and saw that he was looking at my hand to see if there was any blood and then to my face to see if there was any pain. After what seemed like a full five minutes, he conceded that round to the Lord and turned off the machine. He looked at me, then shook his head in wonder, and said, "Your fingers should have been crushed or sheared right off." And that was all that was said about it. I looked at the pressure gauge on the machine, which was set at about 78 psi, and I realized that he was right; it only takes about 8 pounds of pressure to crush a human bone.

Why did all of this happen? I believe God sent me there to help this man be fully restored to his relationship with God and to have his faith renewed. You see, his first wife died of cancer. I believe he would have grieved and gotten over her death without difficulty. But what really destroyed his faith was the fact that everybody in the church had been prophesying day and night that she would live and not die.

I don't know what became of this man, but I do know that God performed so many signs, wonders, and miracles for this man while I was working with him that he could not help but realize that even though the words concerning his first

Chapter Three

wife were not from the Lord, the work of the Holy Ghost was not diminished, nor was God's unfailing love for him.

Chapter Four

*A*t this point you may be wondering how I went from being the guy who caused would-be preachers to throw their Bibles in the garbage can to being the preacher working to restore the faith of a wounded brother. That is a good question. It most certainly was through no design of my own.

I would have to say that God really got my full attention when He took hold of my money. It went like this. I had managed to hold a job for around two years, when

Chapter Four

I decided I needed a change. So when my job came to an end and I was laid off, I moved from Regina to Surrey in order to collect UIC benefits and make a new start.

Well, I found it necessary to go on assistance (welfare) until my claim was processed. Oddly enough, or as fate would have it, they put me up in an emergency shelter in New Westminster, a city just across the river. Then I waited. And I waited, and I waited.

When it got to the point where they were six cheques behind, I thought I had waited long enough and that a visit to the local UIC office was in order. They started checking, and then they got a little flustered and told me, "Mr. Peters, we can't tell you what is holding up your file from being processed. We can't even find your file."

I guess at this point they expected me to go ballistic, and it surprised me as well that I didn't get the least bit upset. As I was leaving the office, they said they would look into it and call me the minute they found out anything.

It was a nice spring day, so I made my way home and sat on the front steps of the motel where I was now staying. I let my mind wander aimlessly for a while, and then it hit me out of the blue. I would not see those cheques until I promised to stop running from God. When I got this realization, I told Him, "OK, You win. Just give me my money." I was pretty sure He had heard me, because the next morning I found all six cheques in my mailbox.

Chapter Four

Not long after this, a friend introduced me to a church that was sponsoring a soup kitchen once a week. I felt somehow that God wanted me to accept Jesus and invite Him to live in my heart. Now, that would have been fine on its own, but I knew that human beings had had a hand in writing the Bible, and I wasn't prepared to put any faith in something written by the hand of man. So, I explained to the Lord that this for me was a real sticking point.

Later that night after I went to bed, I had a dream, the details of which I can't communicate just now, except for the voice that spoke to me saying, "Be not afraid, for the promise is there."

This, of course, told me that no matter what man had done with God's Word, it still had enough truth and virtue to be trusted and depended on. Today, nearly thirty years later, I am convinced that God esteems His Word above all else. Though heaven and the earth should pass away, God's Word will stand forever.

Chapter Five

When I preach, I notice that sometimes even while I am still speaking people will leave their seats and start coming to the altar area. At this point, I begin to realize that God has already worked in the hearts of the people and that His Holy Spirit is ready to take the service in a different direction. I am wondering, are you someone who does not yet know God but have been reading this book and you suddenly realize, "This is for me. I need this Jesus in my life. I need to turn everything over to God and make a new start"? Are you someone who has said yes to God and lived no? Are you someone who has lost your way or maybe, for whatever reason, lost your faith but feel God knocking at the door of your heart?

I want to take this opportunity to give you a chance to receive Christ Jesus into your heart. I want to give you a chance to give it all over to God. I want to give you a chance to come home to God, to give Him everything that's wrong and let Him make it right. Will you say this prayer in your heart?

> Dear Lord Jesus, I need You in my life. I have life in the natural, but I am spiritually dead. The nature

Chapter Five

of sin has kept me apart from the one true God and You, Lord Jesus, whom He has sent. You came into this world and died in my place so that You could give me Your life and make me a new person on the inside.

You died, and You rose from the dead and went back into heaven, where You sit at the right hand of almighty God, so that You could send the Holy Spirit to dwell within me and give me the strength and wisdom to live this new life.

Lord Jesus, please take away all of my sinful nature and give me in its place your righteous nature. Help me to work out my own salvation with a right heart and a right attitude.

Forgive me, Lord, and wash me clean. Fill me with your Holy Spirit, and lead me to a good church, where I can learn all that I need to learn about this new life and then fulfill Your purpose for my life.

I believe that You have heard me, Jesus, and that You have not rejected me but have received me gladly and that I am even now a brand-new person and that the sinful nature, which I have turned my back on, no longer has any power over me. Thank You, Lord Jesus, that because of You, I am a new creation. Amen.

Chapter Five

Now, if you said this prayer and you really meant every word, then you are saved and will not need to say this prayer again and again. Once is enough. One last word: don't think that because you have turned your life over to Jesus that you will never have any problems from now on. You will still have difficulties and trials; the difference is that now you will have God walking through them with you. God has always loved you. He will never leave you or forsake you.

So, two questions should now be on your heart: "What just happened?" and "Now what do I do?" Well, let's look at the words you just prayed. The nature of sin has been like a permanent wedge between you and God. By turning your life over to Jesus and asking him to forgive your sin, that wedge has been removed; and from now on, God, through the person of His Holy Spirit, will walk with you, for as long as you live. The blood of Jesus has washed you clean. You have been, in effect, born again, and the Holy Spirit will work in your heart and life to develop in you the nature of Jesus Christ. It usually takes time and seldom happens overnight.

You asked God to lead you to a church where you can learn everything that you will need to know about this new life He has given you. That means that if your friends and family won't go to church with you, you keep going to church anyway. It means that no matter what people say or do, you never go back to the lifestyle that

Chapter Five

you have left but keep walking forward into the will of God.

You are human. You are not perfect yet, and you will make mistakes. When you make a mistake, you simply ask God to forgive you and to help you not to keep making the same mistakes. In truth, it is like learning to walk and talk all over again. This is working out your salvation with a right heart and a right attitude.

The nature of sin no longer has a right to control you. You have a choice. God has a plan and a purpose for your life. You have been adopted into the family of God. That is why you go to church. Everything in your life has just changed. God is in the process of making you his son or daughter. That means a new lifestyle and new friends. It means a new way of thinking. It means that you have new rights and privileges. Church is where we learn what all of that means and how to keep it all. There is more that I could say, but this is enough for now.

Chapter Six

This is exactly what happened in my life. I got saved, or was born again. I turned my back on my old lifestyle. I said good-bye to my old friends and never looked back. I went to church and learned what I needed to learn about my new lifestyle. I learned what God's purpose for my life was, and I learned to follow His direction.

I read all of the Kenneth E. Hagin books. I learned how to be led of the Holy Spirit. I learned what gifts the Holy

Spirit had placed within me and how to be used by God. It took a few years, but in 1991 I made a decision to train and prepare for the full-time ministry. I went to Bible school. I played in the church band, ran errands, cleaned the sanctuary, and prayed for people who phoned the prayer line.

Things began to happen right from the first night. A man in northern Alberta had watched the TV telecast and phoned in to pray that his son would get saved and live for God. We prayed together, and the Holy Spirit told me that He needed to get saved also. So I asked him if he was ready to accept Christ also, and he said yes. So I led him through the sinner's prayer. Then the Holy Spirit showed me that he had severe back pain. When

Chapter Six

I asked him about it, he said that he had been a crane operator for twenty years and that the doctors could do nothing for him except give him painkillers. I prayed with him for healing, and immediately he was set free from the pain.

The next caller was a woman from northern British Columbia. She called in to get some relief from arthritis. I began to pray, and all of a sudden I could hear her daughter getting all excited in the background. "Mom!" she was almost yelling. "Look at your hand!" She had arthritis so bad that her hand was literally curled or frozen like a claw. As soon as I began to minister in the Holy Ghost, the crippling disease began to leave, and her hand opened up, and she was free.

One night a lady who sounded like she was eighty or ninety years old phoned the prayer line. Her first words to me were these: "I think I've broken my back. Could you pray for me?"

Well, I began to pray earnestly, and all of a sudden the phone went quiet. Then I could hear her walking back and forth shouting, "Hallelujah! Hallelujah!" She came back to the phone a couple minutes later, saying, "When you began to pray, I felt two bones go back in place. Thank you." And then she just hung up.

Another lady phoned in during a morning service, saying "I don't believe you people are from God. I think you are all false prophets and charlatans! But if you can do anything, please help me."

Chapter Six

It was clear that this woman had faith in God, or else she was just desperate for help, or both. I started by asking what the trouble was, and she told me that she suffered incurable, intolerable back pain. I prayed with her for a moment or two, and she was marvelously set free of the pain!

I had been helping and leading worship for a small church. Then one day in 1996 the pastor had me ordained, moved the church into Regina, Saskatchewan, and stepped down, leaving me as pastor of the church. I pastored this church for several years, and then one day the Holy Spirit told me to close the church and start to do the work of an evangelist.

Since then, I have ministered in many places in western Canada, and I have some wonderful testimonies to share in the following pages.

Chapter Seven

*I*n March of 2009, my wife went to visit her family in South Korea. We had met two years earlier, while working with some of the local missions in the downtown east-side area of Vancouver.

They say that God moves in mysterious ways. My wife, Karen, had worked for fifteen years on the mission field, in China, Africa, and various other places. We realized one day that God had allowed us to meet and fall in love, and so we began to make plans for our marriage. While my future wife was visiting her friends and family, she began to talk to one of her many friends in the ministry. There had been so much excitement about the work I had been doing that within a month the church had sent me the money for a return-trip ticket to the city of Seoul.

On my first day there, my fiancée and I met with the pastor of the church, and then we were whisked away to a wonderful restaurant for brunch. Here we met two other pastors and a young woman who was to serve as my interpreter for several meetings. This was a young woman who had been studying in the United States and had recently returned to stay with her family for the summer. I mention her now, because she would

Chapter Seven

---

later be filled with the Holy Spirit and return to the United States.

After a wonderful lunch and a lengthy discussion of where to hold conferences, how long they should be, etc., we were hurried off in the same black limo that had taken us to the restaurant to a theatre for a movie. Then it was back again home for an impromptu healing service. The Holy Spirit spoke into the situations of some of the pastors who were present, and the woman who was acting as our chauffeur reported that God had touched her and she was now hearing out of an ear that had been deaf for years.

We had a couple days to see the city, and then it was time to minister at the Sunday church service. There was a good turnout, and the pastor gave a good message. After the customary communion service, I was introduced, and the meeting was turned over to me.

God spoke into the lives of many who were there, and then a young boy, maybe five or six years old, was brought to me for healing. His nurse had dropped him as a baby, and he had been autistic ever since. The parents, I was told, were not Christians, but if God were to heal their son, they would believe and turn their lives over to Christ.

Well, I began to minister, and the Holy Ghost spoke to me and said that He would do a slow work in healing this boy, so that it would not be overwhelming. That was a year ago. At last report, the boy was recovering just as the Holy Ghost had said he would.

Chapter Seven

This young boy's grandfather also came up for healing. He was deaf in one ear and asked if Jesus could heal him. Within moments God had touched him and opened his ear so that he could hear clearly.

After this meeting, we went from church to church and house to house, ministering in the gift of the word of knowledge and in the gift of the word of prophecy. Within two weeks, people were coming from many different provinces to receive what the Holy Spirit had for them.

By this time, the church and family had completed their plans for our wedding, and one of the church members opened his home on a private resort for the ceremonies. As a result, we had a wonderful wedding under a clear, blue sky, and everything went perfectly.

We had the next week to ourselves, and then it was back to business. First, there was a meeting at the Selah House, and then we went to Cher Won, just a few miles from the North Korean border, and then it was south again to Seoul for a three-day conference.

After this, there was a lot of traveling. We started with a two-day conference in Daejeon city, then we went to the city of Young San for two days. After that, it was back to Seoul and then to Sosan city on the western coast. During this time, people were healed of paralysis, diabetes, and cancer. They were filled with the Holy Spirit, received money miracles, and so much more.

Chapter Seven

I used to ask myself, "What does it matter if I get saved or not?" Well, if God had not personally intervened in my life, I would have perished long ago, and none of these things would have happened to or through me. I thank God that He had a plan for my life, and I know that He has a plan for yours as well.

In closing, I feel I need to touch once more on the prophetic ministry. There is not enough teaching, I think, on the prophetic. There are those who have the gift of the word of prophecy, but they are not true prophets. There are those who have the gift of tongues and interpretation of tongues. As we know from Scripture, these two gifts used in their proper setting, add up to prophecy—but the speakers do not stand in the office of the prophet.

Someone once asked why I teach that there is a difference between the prophet and prophecy. Quite simply, one who is used in the gift of the word of prophecy simply gives a message under the unction of the Holy Spirit. In this person's lifetime, God may use him or her only once or twice to give a word of prophecy. This does not make that person a prophet.

Someone who stands in the office of the prophet has a lifetime responsibility to God and His people. When an apostle, for example, plants a church and chooses the leadership, he calls for the prophets to come and confirm these appointments. It takes twenty years or more for a prophet to be fully trained by

Chapter Seven

the Holy Spirit. Someone with the gift of the word of prophecy may not have had any training at all. One does not just wake up one morning and announce to the world, "Today, I have become a prophet!" That is done by the Holy Spirit speaking through the pastor, and that will happen two or more times. Remember that in the witness of two or three will the truth be established.

This was the case with me. God opened a door for me to speak at one church, and as I was walking back to my seat, the Holy Spirit spoke through the pastor and said, "Brother John, today you have confirmed your ministry as a prophet and teacher." This was repeated a few months later at a different church about an hour away from the first, and so my election to the office of the prophet was confirmed in public by the Holy Spirit.

Someone might ask, "Well, if you're a prophet, what have you prophesied?" That is a fair question, but there were several men whom the Word of God calls "prophets" who never uttered one single prophecy. Job and John the Baptist are two of these men. So from this we see that there are also different types of prophets, but that is for another book.

During the course of my first visit to South Korea, my party and I were given a tour of an observation tower overlooking the Demilitarized Zone. There the Holy Spirit showed me many things and had me tell the commander that many big guns were being aimed at his outpost.

Chapter Seven

Over the course of the next two years, the Holy Spirit spoke to me about the attack on the island of Yeon Pyoung, the imminent death of North Korean leader Kim Jung II, and a shift in power that came to pass within six months. The Bible tells us that there are two ways to judge the accuracy of a prophetic message. One is if what is spoken and or written comes to pass. We will discuss the other in another book at another time.

Part Two

Taking the Right Exit

Chapter Eight

So, then, welcome back. While "A Divine Intervention" has served as an appetizer, "Taking the Right Exit" will prove to be the main course. I enjoyed being able to share my experiences and testimonies, and many have been asking—or rather strongly suggesting—that I pick up the pen once more and offer a second work on Christian living. In an effort then to please and appease, let's get started.

From looking at my opening statement, one might get the idea that I have food on my mind from the outset. I am, in fact, reminded of the past year that my wife Karen and I spent in Seoul, South Korea.

We began speaking to some of our friends from the area in the few months preceding our trip at the end of March 2011. Some of our Korean friends and associates so enjoyed our previous visit in 2009 that they thought to continue the work that we had begun together by having a series of conferences in the area surrounding the city of Seoul.

I have to say here that the Korean people are wonderful hosts, and the food is always fresh and wonderfully delicious. Much as in many other nations, food

Chapter Eight

seems to be at the center of the social aspect of Korean culture.

At the start, there was talk of having some forty or fifty new churches in the area that were excited about these conferences. Needless to say, I was more than a little interested in this offer, and yet something didn't feel right somehow. So when the money was released for my wife and me to purchase the airline tickets, I made sure that God was in this thing with us.

I learned early in my walk with Jesus that if you don't have the peace, pray! I couldn't say exactly why I felt a little uneasy about this trip, but the feeling wouldn't leave me; so I made sure that I talked to God before we paid for the tickets.

Well, I prayed a few times, and the answer always came back: "Just go. I'll tell you what to do when you get there." This response to my prayer both assured me that we were to go and warned me that not everything would go according to plan. But that's the thing, isn't it? All too often we make elaborate plans and then expect God to bless them. It's not surprising that God said in the Word not to boast by saying we will go to this city, do business for a year, and become wealthy (James 4:13).

There it was: Go, but don't be presumptuous. That was enough for me. All I really needed was for God to say, "Go," because I knew then that He would look after my wife and me. Now I had the peace, and we could buy the tickets

Chapter Eight

and put everything in storage, which is exactly what we did. I arranged for a leave of absence from my job, dealt with all the utilities, and moved everything to a storage complex in Surrey, British Columbia. Even though we started making plans well in advance, we still had barely enough time to get everything done. We were busy pretty much right up until flight time.

It honestly felt good to be boarding the Korean Air flight At YVR in Vancouver. Everything went smoothly, and we were on board the plane and in the air before we knew it. We were finally able to relax, and we arrived at Incheon Airport rested and ready for whatever God had prepared for us.

That is always a comfort for me. If God sends a person somewhere, He always gets in the details and works everything out. It was no surprise, then, to be met at the airport by one of the pastors we had been talking with. We were whisked off to a nearby hotel for several hours of one-on-one ministry with a group of local pastors and ministers.

We were kept rather busy for the next day or two; and then our accommodations were changed, and we were able to take things at a much slower pace. We had a day of ministry in Seoul, and then went south to the Dongtan area, where we would stay for the next two months.

In spending time with some of the acquaintances we had made in 2009, I could sense a tangible difference in the

Chapter Eight

way they were relating to us, and so I began to understand my reticence prior to our departure from Canada. Within a week or ten days, it got to the point that we felt it best to break fellowship with one group and to proceed cautiously. When I asked the Lord if we should go back to Vancouver after our first conference, He just said, "No. I will tell you what to do."

Over the following two months, then, we visited friends and family and made the best decisions that we could at the time. Well, the year passed quickly, and we renewed some old friendships and made some new friends. We got to know the city of Seoul quite well and kept busy enough to make the time go by faster than we had expected.

We saw God do some wonderful things, as He confirmed His word with signs and wonders following. Broken hearts were mended, the sick were healed, and many who were oppressed by the enemy were set free. It was really a wonderful and restful year.

Now, you might be asking, "When is he going to tell me what God told him to do?" Well, it took a while for me to sort that out, but in the end God put it on my heart to write about Christian living. So here we are looking for the right exit to get onto the King's Highway.

I want to start this work by talking to the new believer, and then we will go on from there and see where the Holy Spirit will take us. So buckle up, get comfortable, and enjoy the ride.

Chapter Nine

So ... you gave your heart to God through His Son Jesus. You turned your back on your old life. But what comes next? The answer, of course, will depend on the circumstances of your salvation. Where did you make the decision to follow Christ and turn your life over to him? This knowledge could have a huge impact on your future happiness. If you were attending church services, stay at that church, if you are comfortable. If you don't feel comfortable, then don't worry about joining a church just yet.

One of the most important things to learn as a new believer is that the written Word of God is the final authority on any given topic. Remember that heaven and earth will pass away, but God's Word will stand forever (Isaiah 40:8). There are so many versions of the truth out there, each one saying, "Follow me!" This creates much controversy and division in the body of Christ, or, in other words, the modern church.

Jesus said it in this way, "Enter through the narrow gate. For wide is the gate and broad is the road that leads to destruction, and many enter through it. But small is the gate, and narrow the road that leads

Chapter Nine

to life, and only a few find it" (Matthew 7:13-14 NIV).

OK, you are probably wondering why Jesus said this and what it all might mean. Many could give you a two-hour teaching on these verses, and in the end your head would be spinning, and you would be wondering what the preacher had been talking about. But it is really not difficult if we try to keep it simple, and that for now would be a good rule of thumb for all of us to follow. Maybe the easiest way to understand this is to compare it to driving on the freeway as you come to a major city. Rather than trying to navigate through the city center with all of the traffic lights and congested traffic, the majority of drivers ahead of you will take the first major bypass they can find, taking an alternate route.

This is what Jesus was really talking about. You see, He has our individual lives all mapped out for us, and He has given us the Holy Spirit to navigate for us as we find our way to his kingdom. Jesus is saying to as many who will listen, "Don't follow the crowd! They are following the wrong map and have no idea where they are going! Don't be afraid; I will show you the right exits."

The following are the instructions I give to everyone to whom I introduce Jesus. I have done the best I could to make them simple enough that even a child could follow them. These directions will lead you to a happy and prosperous

Chapter Nine

relationship with God in heaven, who has now adopted you.

Now that you are "saved," many people will begin to push and pull you in many different directions. "Oh," they will say, "you need to come this way!" or "Oh, you have to go that way!" Sorry to say, they will drag you from one church to another, making you feel like a hamster in a wheel, running and running until you fly off into a ditch somewhere.

Yes, it is good for us to have a home church, where we can make new friends and learn all about living the Christian life. But how do you find a good church? How do you find the right church?

I don't know if you have been to Seoul, a city of some five million people, but there are signs everywhere you look! Here in

North America, you can say to someone, "Meet me at the coffee shop on such and such a street," and eventually your friend will find you without much difficulty. In Seoul, you need to be far more specific. Why? Simply because there are twenty or thirty coffee shops on almost every block in the downtown area. Finding the right church can be like that.

So, then, for what it is worth, a little orientation is in order, I think. Before you start looking for a good church, or the right church, you first need to have some basic knowledge of what the Christian life is about and what the right church should look like.

I like to start everyone off on the right foot. Before you read anything else, read chapter 8 of the book of Romans, which is

Chapter Nine

found in the New Testament of the Bible. Maybe you will ask, "Well, shouldn't I get a Bible first?" Not necessarily, and we will talk about Bibles in just a few minutes. I will quote the excerpts from the book as we go so that you are not losing the flow of this teaching.

First of all, the book of Romans is what was called an epistle, a letter of instruction and information. This particular book was a letter of instruction to the believers who were called the Church in Rome and was written by the apostle Paul. If you want to know, the apostle Paul wrote most of the books in the New Testament and was used by God to establish the church outside of the nation of Israel. You will learn all about him later on, but let me copy this chapter for you before we go any further.

Therefore, there is now no condemnation for those who are in Christ Jesus, because through Christ Jesus, the law of the Spirit of life set me free from the law of sin and death. For what the law was powerless to do in that it was weakened by the sinful nature, God did by sending his own Son in the likeness of sinful man to be a sin offering. And so he condemned sin in sinful man, in order that the righteous requirements of the law might be fully met in us, who do not live according to the sinful nature but according to the Spirit.

Romans 8:1-4 (NIV)

Chapter Nine

These first four verses speak to the heart of the matter. In order for us to understand "the sinful nature," we need to put a bookmark here and turn to the book of Genesis, chapter 1, which is right at the start of the Bible.

Through no design of my own, I find that this is a good opportunity for me to introduce you to the Bible, if you are not already familiar with this book. First, and most important, God is the Author of the Bible from cover to cover. Try not to be distracted by the fact that He used many "ghost writers" in the process.

Many people believe that the story begins in the book of Genesis. That is not entirely accurate. While it records the beginning of life as we know it, this chapter actually is somewhere in the middle of the story.

As you read the Bible from cover to cover, you will begin to see hints of another aspect of creation. The truth is that in the beginning, the kingdom of God consisted of God and the angels. Things apparently were going along pretty smoothly until Lucifer, the angel in charge of the praise and worship team in heaven, became proud and envious and wanted to take what did not belong to him.

And so, as you will read later on, there was war in heaven, and one third of the angels followed Lucifer (who became known as Satan) in rebellion against God; and they were cast out of heaven.

Now, in the process of all of this, the earth was destroyed by a great flood. This

Chapter Nine

is where we pick up the story in the first chapter of the first book of the Bible. You see, the earth had to be a very special place in God's eyes. The first few chapters tell us how the Spirit of God brooded over the water that covered the whole earth.

First, we see that God spoke everything into existence. He made a division in the waters, dividing the waters above from the waters below. The waters above the earth he called heaven, and the water below the division, he called seas. But now I am getting ahead of the story, or perhaps I should say stories.

You see, at face value, the Bible is an interesting collection of stories. It is in fact, a complete library. The first five books make up what is called a legal section.

Then there are twelve books that make up the history section. After this, there is a poetry section, followed by another seventeen books that make up a supernatural or spiritual-life section, for a total of thirty-nine books in the Old Testament. This is mirrored in the twenty-seven books that make up the New Testament.

More than a library, or a collection of books and stories, the Bible is the written will of God. In other words, the heart and mind of God are revealed within these pages: ho He is, where He lives, what He loves and hates, His plans and purposes, and so much more. It is, in fact, the greatest how-to book ever written.

So the book begins with the account, or story, of how God created life on earth, how He made man, and also how we

Chapter Nine

began to keep a record of time. First, God separated the waters, and the evening and the morning were the first day. God gathered the waters together and commanded the dry ground to appear, and the evening and the morning were the second day.

And so God continued in this way for five days, preparing a safe environment for the man whom He would make as the final touch in His creation, or rather, re-creation of the earth. He made the seas and the earth, the grass and the herbs and the fruit-bearing trees, the fowls of the air, the fish of the seas, and every creeping thing by the word of His mouth.

Man, however, was not spoken into existence. Instead, the Bible tells us that God formed man from the dust of the earth with His own hands. Man was made both in the image and the likeness of God. That means that man was made to look just like God on the outside and to be just like God on the inside. Man is also the only creature in all of creation that had the breath of life (the Holy Spirit) breathed into his nostrils by God Himself.

Now, everything went well until the enemy (Satan) tried to spoil what God had made so that he could steal it. He deceived the man and the woman and usurped man's authority in the earth. Man was deceived by Satan, and he and the woman disobeyed God; and the nature of sin entered into all of mankind. Only by turning to God through Jesus Christ can we be set free from the nature of sin.

Chapter Nine

That being said, we can now go on a little farther.

We can see that in the beginning everything that was made was good in God's eyes. The trouble came in through the presence of the serpent in the garden. It is commonly accepted that the serpent was, in fact, Lucifer. He had been kicked out of heaven, but his purpose was still to kill, steal, and destroy everything that man was meant to have.

There is no question that man was meant to be the god of this world. There is enough evidence to show that this is what God intended from the beginning. But when Adam and his wife were deceived in the garden the serpent, our great enemy Lucifer, usurped man's position and authority and kept it until the coming of Jesus Christ.

What follows this event is a long series of events and relationships between God and man that form the history and the teachings of the Old Testament. Five books of law, twelve books of history, five books of poetry, and seventeen books of prophecy, and then God was silent for a period of about four hundred years. But I am getting ahead of myself.

Through the disobedience of man in the garden, the nature of sin entered into all humanity everywhere. And this is what we are talking about in the New Testament: the nature of sin that is inherent in all mankind. Until the birth, death, and resurrection of the Lord Jesus

Chapter Nine

Christ, the blood of animals was used to cover the sins of mankind.

But the blood of animals could never make atonement for sin. Only the blood of Jesus could make atonement for our sins and set us free from the power of sin. It has been said that God knew from the beginning that He would have to shed His own blood for the redemption of man.

Jesus' death and resurrection set us free from the law of sin and death and brought us under the law of grace. As the Scripture says, mercy and truth have met together (Psalm 85:10). And so we find ourselves on the threshold of a new beginning. Old things have passed away, and man has been born again; that is to say, those who have accepted the Lord Jesus Christ have been born again and have received the Spirit of adoption, which is the Holy Spirit.

This should give us enough to go on with the diversified business. "For they that are after the flesh do mind the things of the flesh; but they that are after the Spirit, the things of the Spirit" (Romans 8:5). In other words, this is a bit. If people walk after the flesh, they are careful about natural things. But if they walk after the Holy Spirit, they are careful about spiritual things.

"For to be carnally minded is death; but to be spiritually minded is life and peace" (Romans 8:5). Now what does that mean? The Bible says it in this way: "There is a way that seems right to a man, but in the end it leads to death" (Prov. 14:12 NIV). So, then, our natural mind is unproductive and in the end leads us nowhere. But if we are spiritually minded, our thought life is productive, and we have peace.

Because the carnal mind is enmity against God: for it is not subject to the law of God, neither indeed can be. So then they that are in the flesh cannot please God. But ye are not in the flesh but in the Spirit, if so be that the Spirit of God dwell in you. Now if any man have not the Spirit of Christ, he is none of his" (Romans 8:7-9). So, if we are naturally minded, we cannot please God.

Let's say that a different way. The things of God are spiritually discerned, and the natural mind cannot comprehend them. In other words, if we try to serve God with the natural mind, we are unproductive and frustrated because we cannot understand the things of God. If it were not for the Holy Spirit, it would be impossible to please God. It is no wonder then that we are told to have our minds renewed by the washing of the water of the Word (Ephesians 5:26).

What does that mean to us? It means quite simply that we should read as much of the Word as we possibly can from day to day. It does not matter if we understand what we read, so long as we read. In the process of reading the Word of God, our minds are washed and renewed, making it possible for us to begin to understand the things of God. When I first got saved and began to live this Christian life, my friends used to tell me that I was being brainwashed. And though they did not understand what they were saying, in a

Chapter Nine

sense they were right. My mind was being washed and renewed by the simple act of reading the Bible.

The Bible is a wonderful book that is filled with many interesting stories, which makes it easy to just read and read and read and read. One of the best hints that anyone can give us to help us with this Christian life is simply this: do not be in a hurry. That will make things much easier. God is not in a hurry, and we should not be either. Jesus is the Author and the Finisher of our faith. That means that Jesus knows exactly where we are, where He is taking us, and the best road to get us there. Please remember, you are not in this alone.

All of this has been to say that this is a new beginning and a new direction in your life. As a result, you need to learn all about this new direction and all that it entails. To help you toward that end, Jesus has given you His Holy Spirit, the Word of God, which is the Bible, the church, and something that will become known to you as the fivefold ministry. Quite simply, the fivefold ministry refers to the leadership of the church: pastors and teachers, evangelists, and so on. These are people God has trained and set over the church to teach us how to read the map.

Let's move on to Romans 8:10: "And if Christ be in you, the body is dead because of sin; but the Spirit is life because of righteousness." This would be a good place to ask, "What does that mean?" It means that we are dead to the nature of sin and no longer under its control. We

Chapter Nine

are now alive to God and have been born of the Holy Spirit, having the righteousness of Christ. This does not mean that we are now perfect, but it does mean that we have been adopted into the family of God. So, we are dead to our old life and have a brand-new beginning ahead of us.

And so once again, all of this is to say that life for you, the new believer, will be different from anything you have experienced so far. You will learn to see differently and think differently, having a whole new perspective on life.

There are many things in the book of Romans that we could touch on, such as blessings in Christ, various laws, and things that the law could not do. We could talk about the reasons that Christ was without sin, or we continue to contrast the flesh and the Spirit life. We could talk about the twelve blessings of the Holy Spirit, or the seven things that man can do again, or the seven things that man should not do again.

The book of Romans, or rather chapter 8 of the book of Romans, is a good place for the new believer to get some idea of what is to come, to gain an understanding of the changes that are about to take place in his or her life. The purpose of this book is not to teach you everything you need to know overnight. Rather, it is my hope that the new believer will gain a basic understanding of what the Christian life should be, or what it should look like. And the apostle Paul gives us a clear picture of that in this chapter.

Chapter Nine

There are some other areas that we need to look at also. One such area is what our basic belief should be. Another important area is prayer. What is prayer? Why should we pray? What should we pray for? So to achieve our purpose in preparing the new believer for a happy and productive relationship with God, we will look at the Apostles' Creed and the Lord's Prayer.

Chapter Ten

There are so many voices in the world today, all shouting, "Follow me! I know the way!" All of them are saying, "I have the truth!" There are the Catholics, the Anglicans, the Baptists, the Pentecostals, and many more. Each of these groups have a form of the truth, but they also have their own separate and distinct perspective on the Word of God.

Our purpose is not to say this one is right and that one is wrong but rather to

Chapter Ten

give the believer the same foundation that all of these groups share. Once you have a solid foundation, or basic understanding of the truth, you can choose what is best for you. But for now let's go on to Christian Life 101.

The Apostles' Creed quite simply indicates the doctrine of the twelve apostles of Jesus Christ. As you will note, there were several apostles, which indicates just as many unique perspectives on the teachings of Jesus. And yet they all agreed on the basic points or teachings of Jesus.

It is my intention to touch on each of these points so that there will be no confusion as to what each believer should understand as the basic points of faith. So, then, the following is the Apostles'

Creed, or the basic teaching of the apostles of Jesus Christ.

I believe in God the Father Almighty, Maker of heaven and earth. And in Jesus Christ, his only begotten Son, our Lord, who was conceived by the Holy Spirit, born of the Virgin Mary, suffered under Pontius Pilate, was crucified, dead and buried; he descended into hell and on the third day he rose again from the dead; he ascended into heaven and is seated at the right hand of God the father; from thence he shall come to judge the quick and the dead. I believe in the Holy Spirit, the Holy Church, the communion of saints, the forgiveness of sins, the resurrection of the body and life everlasting.

This, then, in a nutshell, is the essence of the New Testament. Everything else expounds upon these topics. This is the basis of the Christian faith, or rather, of faith in Jesus Christ.

Now the first thing we see is the threefold nature or person of God. First, we see Him as God the Father, Creator of heaven and earth. And then we see Him as Jesus Christ, the only begotten Son of God. Then, following that, we see the person of God in the form of the Holy Spirit. And so, while there is only one God, there are three persons in the Godhead. And so the first thing that I wish to do is to get the new believer acquainted with each of these three persons: God the Father, God the Son, and God the Holy Spirit.

Our first questions might be, who is God, what is He like, and what does He want from me? To answer these questions, and any other question you might have about anything at any time, we refer to the Holy Scriptures, otherwise known as the Bible. I suppose that since we have come this far, we should first talk about the Bible.

But what is the Bible, really? Many have said that it is a book written by men simply to be a crutch for society, but is that really true? There have been increasing situations where modern science has proven many points of the Bible to be accurate and true. So then, if sci-

Chapter Ten

ence is proving the Bible to be true in some areas, could it not be said that the entire book is true?

Technically speaking, the Bible is the written Word of God, written by godly men who were inspired by the Holy Spirit. If we take the Bible at face value, we see it is a collection of wonderful stories, and so it is. Yet more than that, it is, in fact, a portable library. It has a legal section, a history section, a poetry section, and even a section on the supernatural or spiritual realms. These sections themselves are like compressed files that contain a great abundance of valuable and important information.

It has been said that we must read a book repeatedly in order to obtain all the information contained within its pages.

We should read it once to get a general overview of the contents and direction of the book. Then, each following time we read the book, we read in order to gain specific information. We can approach the Bible, the written Word of God, in the same manner.

From cover to cover, the Bible is the heart and mind of God written down in black and white. Why? Why would God put His heart and mind in writing? Quite simply, He did this so that man would never have to guess or wonder about these things. Within these pages, God makes it clear and plain what He loves and what He hates. God reveals His heart and His nature; and from any given point in history, God shows us what was, what is, and what is to come.

Chapter Ten

Many people say that the Bible is just a book, and yet this ordinary book contains the answers to any question mankind can ask about love or life. And people say it's just a book? It is interesting to note that God esteems His Word above all else. The Bible tells us that heaven and earth will pass away but the Word of God will stand forever. That being said, let's continue.

In the opening verses of the Gospel of John, we read the following.

> In the beginning was the Word, and the Word was with God, and the Word was God. ... All things were made by him; and without him, was not any thing made that was made.

In him was life; and the life was the light of men.

> John 1:1, 3-4

This may seem confusing to many, but as we continue, it will make more sense. First of all, to say, "in the beginning" throws us off a little bit if we do not understand the language of the Bible. "In the beginning" does not mean in the beginning of time, or at the beginning of all things. It is to say, in the beginning of our understanding, or from our earliest recollections. Why do I say that? Mostly because God existed before the earth was formed and before any form of life existed on the earth.

Jesus, the Son of God, has many names. One of His names, is the Alpha

Chapter Ten

and the Omega. Simply put, this means, the beginning and the end. So, all things began with Jesus, and they will end with Jesus.

In the book of Genesis, which means "beginnings," we see the beginning of life on earth as we know it, but in truth it picks up the story somewhere in the middle. We will go into that at another time, but for now we are dealing with man's life and reign on the earth and his relationship with his Creator.

I should take a moment to attempt to clarify an important question in the hearts of many. As I take this ministry where God sends me, inevitably I find somebody, somewhere asking me this question: "If God is all-powerful, and all-knowing, why does He cause so much suffering and injustice in the world?"

The truth is that God does not cause any of this. These things happen because men and women disobey God, reject Him, or the follow the "god of this world." Now this may seem confusing to some. So far we have been talking about one God, the God of heaven and earth. And we have to go back to the beginning of this book to be reminded that man was meant to be the god of this world, but the serpent, who is the devil, deceived the man and usurped his authority on the earth, replacing him as the god of this world.

Contrary to popular belief, it is not the God who made us who causes the pain and suffering of the world. Rather,

Chapter Ten

it is Lucifer, known as Satan, who is our great enemy and the source of the suffering of man. If we are not with God, we are against Him. If we are against Him, we are for the devil, otherwise known as Satan. In other words, if we are not serving God, we are serving the devil.

Satan will always pretend to be our friend, but ultimately his one unfaltering goal is to destroy and kill every man, woman, and child on this earth and to steal everything that is ours. If we turn our back on God, we walk into the hands of the devil, who then begins his work of destruction. As Jesus said in the Gospels, "The thief cometh not, but for steal, and to kill, and to destroy" (John 10:10).

I hope this is sufficient to clarify which god is God and that we can carry on from here. It is not, then, the God of our creation who brings suffering and injustice into the world. But when we turn our back on God or walk away from Him, we are exposed to the will of our enemy, and we are vulnerable and helpless to his hatred of all mankind.

In the book of Exodus, we see Pharaoh essentially asking the question, "What god is God?" (5:2). Again, in the book of Kings, there is some confusion as to which god is the true God. In fact, all through the history of Israel, there is confusion and mystery surrounding the identity of the one true God. Now, perhaps I'm getting ahead of things, and I should give you a quick overview of the Bible and its books.

Chapter Ten

The Bible is divided into two sections, the Old and the New Testaments. The Old Testament begins with the creation story and reports the relationship of God and man. The New Testament concerns itself with the kingdom of God and living as a child of God.

The first five books of the Old Testament are known as the Pentateuch, or the five books of the law. These books in order are Genesis, Exodus, Leviticus, Numbers, and Deuteronomy. This is the legal section of your portable library. Following this section are twelve books that make up the history section. These are as follows: Joshua, Judges, Ruth, 1 and 2 Samuel, 1 and 2 Kings, 1 and 2 Chronicles, Ezra, Nehemiah, and finally Esther.

Next comes the poetry section, which is made up of the following five books: the book of Job, the Psalms, the book of Proverbs, Ecclesiastes, and the Song of Solomon. And finally, we have the writings of the prophets in five major books of prophecy and twelve minor books of prophets. The Major Prophets are Isaiah, Jeremiah, Lamentations, Ezekiel, and Daniel. The twelve Minor Prophets, are as follows: Hosea, Joel, Amos, Obadiah, Jonah, Micah, Nahum, Habakkuk, Zephaniah, Haggai, Zechariah, and Malachi.

The New Testament follows a similar pattern. First, we have the four Gospels of the apostles of Jesus Christ: Matthew, Mark, Luke, and John. They are followed

Chapter Ten

---

by the book of Acts, which is also known as the Acts of the Apostles.

Then we have the letters from the apostle Paul to the churches he established throughout his ministry, as well as to some individuals. These letters are also called epistles. These are the books of Romans, 1 and 2 Corinthians, Galatians, Ephesians, Philippians, Colossians, 1 and 2 Thessalonians, 1 and 2 Timothy, Titus, Philemon, and Hebrews.

Following these are letters written by other apostles. These include; James, 1 and 2 Peter; 1, 2 and 3 John, and the book of Jude. Finally, we have the book of Revelation. We will talk more about these books and their authors and their content at a later time, but for now let's carry on.

We have been talking about the threefold person of God. First, we have God the Father, whose name is holy. Our first real introduction to God the Father, though we met him briefly in the book of Genesis as the friend of Abraham, comes in the book of Exodus in chapter 3. I should point out that the story of Moses and our introduction to God the Father comes some five hundred years after the story of Abraham. Moses, a descendent of one of Abraham's grand- children, was raised as the son of the daughter of Pharaoh, having been hidden in a basket and set up on the river to save him from the commands of Pharaoh, who had said every male Hebrew child should die.

So Moses grew up in the house of Pharaoh and was trained for leadership.

Chapter Ten

Many years later, he discovered the truth of his birth and was subsequently exiled from the land of Egypt.

> Now Moses kept the flock of Jethro his father in law, the priest of Midian: and he led the flock to the backside of the desert, and came to the mountain of God, even to Horeb. And the angel of the Lord appeared unto him in a flame of fire out of the midst of a bush: and he looked, and, behold, the bush burned with fire, and the bush was not consumed. And Moses said, I will now turn aside, and see this great sight, why the bush is not burnt. And when the Lord saw that he turned aside to see, God called

unto him out of the midst of the bush, and said, Moses, Moses. And he [Moses] said, Here am I.

Exodus 3:1-4

And the Lord told Moses not to come any closer but to take off his sandals because he was standing on "holy ground." And He went on to say, "I am the God of thy father, the God of Abraham, the God of Isaac, and the God of Jacob" (Exodus 3:6). And so here, we see God introducing himself to Moses and to us. It is important to note that God is the God of the living and not of the dead. So if we have a good relationship with God, though we leave this earth, we do not die but rather live with Him forever. And we

Chapter Ten

also see that wherever God is, is holy ground.

No God has a conversation with Moses, and tells him it is time for Moses to begin to do the work the Lord had prepared him to do. And the Lord went on to explain things more fully. And in verse 13 Moses says the following: "Behold, when I come to the children of Israel, and shall say unto them, the God of your fathers hath sent me unto you; and they shall say to me, What is His name? what shall I say unto them?"

In other words, Moses was saying, "Just a minute; when I get back to Egypt and talk to your people Israel and say to them, 'The God of your fathers has sent me to you,' and they ask me, 'What is His name?' how should I answer them?"

"And God said unto Moses, I AM THAT I AM: and he said, Thus shalt thou say unto the children of Israel, I AM hath sent me to you" (Exodus 3:14).

In this last statement, God declares His name. And God says it in this way because it describes His nature. The nature and character of God is so vast that the only way to truly describe God is to say, "I am that I am," or "He is that He is." The people of Israel know him as Jehovah. In other places in the Bible, we will come to know him by many other names. Jehovah Nisi, Jehovah Jirah, Father of lights, and the God of heaven and earth, are just a few of his many names.

Perhaps the first time we see mention of the Son of God is in the book of Daniel.

Chapter Ten

Shadrach, Meshach, and Abednego were thrown into a furnace when they disobeyed the king of Babylon. When the king went closer to see if their God could protect them, he said, "I see four men walking loose ... and the form of the is like the Son of God" (Daniel 3:25). Yes, there are other places where the Scriptures make reference to the Son of God but perhaps none so directly. That is to say, perhaps this is the first distinction between God the Father and the Son of God. There is another reference that speaks of the birth of Jesus Christ in the book of the prophet Isaiah. Then in the New Testament, in the four Gospels, we see the birth, life, death, and resurrection of the Lord Jesus Christ. In these four books we get to see much of the work of the Holy Spirit. And so we see the persons of God the Father, God the Son, and God the Holy Spirit.

When Jesus was baptized, we find the three persons altogether in one place and at one time. First, we see Jesus being baptized, and we know Him to be the Son of God. Then, as He comes up out of the water, we see the Holy Spirit descending upon Him in the form of a dove. And then we hear the voice of God the Father, speaking from heaven, and saying, "This is my beloved Son, in whom I am well pleased" (Matthew 3:17).

All three persons of the Godhead play an active role in our salvation. The Holy Spirit draws us to the Lord Jesus Christ, who introduces us to the Father, who then forgives our sin because of the blood of

Chapter Ten

His Son Jesus; and God the Father gives us the spirit of adoption, which is in fact, the Holy Spirit who dwells within us to complete the work of salvation.

Well, that wasn't as intimidating as I thought it might be. Once you read the Gospels and the book of Acts, you will better understand the Apostles' Creed, which is our basic doctrine and the foundation of our faith and walk with God. Everything else is built upon this foundation. It is that simple. Everything else comes through different teachers and their teachings. I remember in my early years as a Christian, things were not laid out so neatly, and there were several years of confusion and uncertainty for me to work through.

But now we come to perhaps my favorite topic in the Bible (apart from the person of Jesus Christ): the subject of prayer. What is prayer? How and when and where does one pray? Well, quite simply, prayer is talking to God. There are many ways to talk to God. You can talk to God just about anywhere and at any time.

There are many forms of prayer, but I love the model prayer Jesus gave to His disciples. This is known to us today as the Lord's Prayer, and it is a wonderful model. One day the disciples said to Jesus, "Teach us to pray" (Luke 11:1). He then gave them a model on which to base all of their conversations with God. It is important to understand how to approach God and also how to speak to Him.

Chapter Ten

Our Father which art in heaven, Hallowed be thy name. Thy kingdom come. Thy will be done in earth, as it is in heaven. Give us this day our daily bread. And forgive us our debts, as we forgive our debtors. And lead us not into temptation, but deliver us from evil: for thine is the kingdom, and the power, and the glory, for ever. Amen.

Matthew 6:9-13

This is the model Jesus gave us regarding prayer. The majority of people pray this prayer in sixty seconds or less. And they really don't get the full benefit of what Jesus is teaching. In order to fully understand, we need to break this down and make it personal.

First of all, He addresses God as "our Father." So the first thing Jesus wants us to see and understand is that God is our Father. Understanding our relationship is the first key to talking with God and should be the basis for every conversation we have with Him. We need to understand that God is not distant from us and that He is never too busy to hear us. Jesus wants us to remember and understand that when we were saved, we received the Spirit of adoption and so have become sons and daughters of the most high God.

So, then, we have this relationship with the King of the universe. Well, that is pretty awesome. How do you approach somebody as awesome as God? I suggest you start with respect, bordering on

Chapter Ten

reverence; and the more reverence, the better. In other words, you start every conversation with God by remembering who you are and who you're talking to.

When I talk to new believers about prayer, I usually say it in this way:

"Well, now what? I said yes to Jesus, and the pastor said I've been adopted, but what does that mean? I guess I'll have to read the Bible to find out what that means." When we read the Scriptures, we learn what it means to be adopted by God. We learn who He is and where He lives.

Then we might begin to think, "So, as a child of God, I have rights, and I have privileges. That's awesome! So now I need to read the Bible again and find out what those rights and privileges are.

'Thy will be done' also means that I have duties and obligations. Hmmm, that's not so awesome. Well, I better read the Bible again and find out what God wants from me."

If we are doing this right, we will have to read the Bible through several times. We will have to read it once to learn what it means to be adopted as a child of God. We will have to read the Bible a second time to find out about where God lives. Then we would read the Bible a third time in order to understand the name of God. So, in just praying the first line of the Lord's Prayer, we are moved to read the Bible three times.

We must read the Bible a fourth time in order to understand God's kingdom. Why do we need to understand this?

Chapter Ten

Because the Word tells us to pray with the spirit *and* the understanding. We need to understand what we are praying so that we can pray in agreement with the Holy Spirit. Now we need to read it twice more, in order to understand the will of God and the relationship between heaven and earth.

"Give us this day our daily bread," we pray. Now, at this time, we are probably asking God, "Why am I praying for bread? I have lots of food at home. My cupboards are full; my fridge and freezer are full. I don't need money; I have a good job. Why am I asking for bread?"

To understand this statement, we need to understand the language of the Bible. Jesus said that healing is the children's bread (Matthew 15:25-28). So then we are not praying for bread or food, but instead we are praying for healing. So we have to read the Bible again to understand healing. And we need to continue in this way to the end of the prayer.

It amazes me that we take something that has so much depth and is so important to understanding the Christian life, and we go through it in sixty seconds or less. The truth is, the Lord's Prayer is not just a model for prayer; it is a discipleship program for every believer.

For example, when we talk about rights and privileges, duties and obligations, we are in fact speaking of covenants and legal contracts with the God of heaven and earth. I find it interesting that many have written about the promises of God, but not really said anything about

Chapter Ten

the obligations. The Bible contains over 850 promises that pertain to each and every believer. Some are conditional, and others are unconditional. If we see it in the proper light, it all leads to relationship with God.

If we have prayed the Lord's Prayer as God meant for us to pray it, and we have understood where God was taking us, we should have read the Bible at least fifteen times, simply to understand five verses of Scripture. Yes, I could say a lot more, but I want to keep this simple and easy to understand.

Chapter Eleven

*I*n order to keep and hold to the most basic and essential truths of the Scriptures, I have glossed over some important topics. But now we have come to that place where I need to go into more detail. I need to talk to you about things like water baptism, the Holy Spirit, and the church.

Up until this point, it has been possible to avoid strong doctrine, and for the most part, all churches and denominations will fully agree with what I have talked about

Chapter Eleven

to this point. While I will do my best to hold to the truth of the Scriptures, different groups will view these topics through the perspective of their own denominations and teachings.

For example, there are many groups today who tell us that the apostles and prophets were only for the time following the ministry of Jesus. They tell us that things have changed and that the church does not need these ministries any longer. They also tell us that the evangelist no longer has a place in the church of Jesus Christ. Why? Because for the most part they have become immoral and untrustworthy, being greedy and preaching the gospel only for money. And they also tell us that there is no distinction between the pastor and the teacher, which leaves the church looking far different from what it should be.

The apostle Paul told us in the New Testament that in the end days there will be many who have a form of godliness but deny the power thereof. In other words, Paul was saying to the church, "In the end days, there will be many who look like the church and talk like the church, but they deny the power of the church." And we see this happening today. I believe this has come about because while knowledge has increased in the earth, understanding seems to have declined. Perhaps understanding has declined because experience also has declined. Yet, this is not entirely the fault of the church.

Chapter Eleven

I say this because false prophets and false teachers seem to be ever increasing in number and popularity, leading many astray. A church is only as good as its leadership, and if the leadership is not fully or properly trained, it is not properly equipped or able to recognize or to deal with the lies of the devil. As a result they begin to say that prophets and apostles are not for the church today.

Another area that is being cut out of the church simply because of a lack of understanding is the gift of speaking in other tongues or languages. Because the Holy Spirit is being rejected by more and more churches, more and more pastors are teaching against the gifts of the Holy Spirit. It seems that increasingly pastors are saying from the pulpit that speaking in tongues is from the devil. They teach the people that it is wrong to use this gift and forbid its use. There are other less obvious areas where the same thing is happening in churches all over this world. So because of fear and ignorance, or in other words, because of fear and the lack of sound teaching, the world is beginning to fear the Holy Spirit.

For this reason, I feel that I need to teach briefly but openly about the Holy Spirit and His gifts. If anyone, no matter what the person's position in the church, tries to tell you that the Holy Spirit and His gifts are not for the church or the believer, remember that the Bible, the written Word of God is the final authority on that. Heaven and earth will pass away, but the Word of God will stand forever.

Chapter Eleven

Water baptism is a very important part of the Christian experience and conversion process. Without water baptism, there is no repentance of sin. Many groups and organizations teach that if you sprinkle an infant with water, then he or she has been water baptized. But this is not entirely accurate.

You might ask, "How can you say that, Brother John?" I can say it because I understand the purpose of water baptism. What is water baptism, and what is its purpose? The Bible tells us that water baptism is for the repentance of sins. This is why the sprinkling of infants with water is ineffective in today's church. We need to understand the purpose of baptism.

As I have already stated, water baptism is for the repentance of sins. So the first question that must be asked is this: How many sins has that baby committed, and how many of his or her sins are being remitted? The answer is simply none and none. The baby has committed no sins; therefore, no sins have been remitted.

The next point we need to look at is the method of baptism. Many churches today teach that the sprinkling of water on the forehead is sufficient to wash away a person's sin. Yet, if we look at the Scriptures, we find that the Word of God talks about the sin nature being buried in the waters of baptism. For me, and for many others, this indicates full-immersion baptism. This is where the nature of sin is put to death and forever buried.

When we read the book of acts, and the story of Cornelius, we can clearly see

Chapter Eleven

the importance of water baptism for the believer. When Cornelius and his household were baptized, they were also filled with the Holy Spirit, with the evidence of speaking in other tongues. As you will see a little later, speaking in other tongues was how the Jewish believers recognized that God had accepted the Gentile believers.

The book of Acts, which follows the Gospel of John, is our off-ramp for this work. In reading through the chapters of the Acts of the Apostles, you will see the situations and circumstances, as well of the development of the church of Jesus Christ. You will also see clearly what today's church should look like and also get an idea of how it should function.

In my next book, God willing, I will open things up more specifically for those who really want to know God and have a strong desire to study and to serve Him in the ministry of the Word. I will teach in greater detail about the promises God makes to the believer and also how to really know Him.

For the new believer, as you have been reading this book, it has served as an introduction, or preparation, for your relationship with God and His Son Jesus Christ and also the Holy Spirit. This is known in some circles as the "honeymoon" stage of our journey, and it usually lasts for a year or two. Please watch for my next book, *After the Honeymoon,* which will be an in-depth look at Christian living and understanding church life.

Chapter Eleven

Here is a final word of advice, if I may call it that: Don't be in a hurry. Enjoy this time as much as possible. After a year or two, you will be really prepared to go farther. Until then, enjoy the salvation experience to the full, and may God bless you as you get to know Him.

CPSIA information can be obtained at www.ICGtesting.com
Printed in the USA
LVOW080711100513

333100LV00001B/4/P